D1787089

Turning the Corner at Dusk

Jacquie Buncel

Turning the Corner at Dusk

Wolsak & Wynn

© Jacquie Buncel, 2010

No part of this publication may be reproduced, stored in a retrieval system or transmitted, in any form or by any means, without the prior written consent of the publisher or a license from The Canadian Copyright Licensing Agency (Access Copyright). For an Access Copyright license, visit www.accesscopyright.ca or call toll free to 1-800-893-5777.

Cover images: The building on the cover photo is the Orthodox synagogue in Prešov, Slovakia. The photo on the back cover is the Memorial to the Martyrs of the Holocaust which is located in the synagogue courtyard.
Author's photograph: Greg van Riel
Cover design: Rachel Rosen
Typset in Garamond Premiere Pro
Printed by Coach House Books Toronto, Canada

The publisher gratefully acknowledges the support of the Canada Council for the Arts, the Ontario Arts Council and the Canada Book Fund for their financial assistance.

Wolsak and Wynn Publishers Ltd.
#102–69 Hughson Street North
Hamilton, ON
Canada L8R 1G5

Library and Archives Canada Cataloguing in Publication

Buncel, Jacquie, 1960-
Turning the corner at dusk / Jacquie Buncel.

Poems.
ISBN 978-1-894987-36-3

I. Title.

PS8603.U53T87 2009   C811'.6   C2009-904106-5

To Erwin and Penny

To Lorraine always

and for Aviva and Maya, the next generation

Turning the Corner at Dusk

I. Waiting for the Unveiling: Journey to Prešov

Journey to Prešov	11
Prešov	13
Return	14
Aryanization	15
Discovering	17
The River	18
The Trains	20
Hiding	21
The Importance of Knowing	22
Resting Ground	23
Unveiling	24
Haviva Reik	25
Aunt Marta	27
(Ap)peal	28
Departure	30
Epilogue – Reunion of Jews from Prešov	31

II. Turning the Corner at Dusk

Birth, December 1960	35
Snapshot	37
Henriette	38
Memory, 1972	40
Therapy	42
Turning the Corner at Dusk	43
Herbie	45
Nuclear Family Panic	46
Children of Holocaust Survivors	48

Memorial, Paris	50
Amsterdam Jewish Museum	52
Autumn Reflection	55
Yom Kippur in Kensington Market	56
Journey to the Funeral of Lois Heitner (1957–1993)	59
Epiphany by Chikanishing Creek	61
Seesaw	62
In the Closet with my Relatives on the French Riviera	64

III. The Oceans Part and Out You Come

Wishing for a Child	69
Aviva	70
My Body Has Turned Utilitarian	73
Attachment	75
Diaper Rash	76
Bath Time	78
Mapping	79
Maya	81
Excavating Again	82
A Tribute to Marta Buncel by Erwin Buncel	83
Family	84
Whining	85
The Beach at Sandbanks Park	86
Generation to Generation	88
Evocation	89
December Hope	90
Piano Music	91
Divining	93
Historical Notes	95
Notes on the Poems	97
Glossary of Terms and Phrases	100
Acknowledgements	102

I

Waiting for the Unveiling: Journey to Prešov

Prešov pronounced "preshov"

Unveiling: A Jewish custom of unveiling the tombstone in the first eleven months following the death. A cloth is taken off the tombstone to reveal the inscription and prayers are sung and recited by family and friends.

Journey to Prešov

It took my father forty-eight years
to come back.

Two flights and one overnight train
stopping in every village and town
crowded with people speaking languages
we don't understand.

A woman and a man help
put our bags above the berths
as we all bunk down for the night.

Nervously we sleep as
the train bumps along.
I listen to ocean waves
and Debussy on my walkman,
the Tatras cocooning the train
as it winds through the countryside.

When morning breaks,
one small town after another.
We watch out of the open window
for Kysak, and our next train,
dusty air blowing in our faces.

Minutes on that train
and we're there.
Prešov
I've wondered about you, birthplace of my father.

It was only ten years ago
I learned you existed,
a town in the far eastern reaches of Slovakia,

only an accent betraying my father,
when questioned, he would look pointedly away.

Now he looks eagerly around.
A boy trying to recognize
and I observe,
waiting for the unveiling.

Prešov

Two churches on the main street:
one fourteenth-century Catholic cathedral
and one seventeenth-century Protestant church.
a military base
a university
one art gallery
shops with overpriced watches and electronics
a liquor store
boutiques selling wool dresses and rayon blouses
two hotels, the Šariš and the Dukla
the Jonas Zaborsky Theatre
one shopping plaza
one bakery
five restaurants
six Jewish cemeteries
(only one in use)
four synagogues
(only one in use)
one Holocaust memorial.

Return

On Saturday morning
we walk through the courtyard
to reach the yellow-mortar synagogue.
My father pulls open the heavy black door tentatively.
A man comes to the door, looks at us suspiciously.
"You are Jewish?" he asks in Yiddish.
My father nods and points at his chest.
"I'm from Prešov"
he answers proudly
and somehow I understand him.

The man grabs his hand,
pulls him inside quickly,
leads us to a small room at the back of the sanctuary
where fifteen men are *davening*,
swaying as they recite the morning prayers.
Suddenly we are surrounded.
A native son has returned.
Everyone is chattering in Yiddish.
Lost is the drone of the man leading the service.
Mr. Landa is from before
and Mr. Rochlitz.
Mr. Kolbar remembers my grandfather and my aunt.
They pull out cake and a bottle.
I eat the *lekech* and sip the sweet brandy.
My father is beaming.

Aryanization

Ordinance 63	declares who is a Jew. restricts the number of Jewish lawyers, doctors.
Law No. 113	liquidates Jewish businesses.
Law 46/1940	transfers Jewish farmland to non-Jews.
Constitutional Law 210/40	bars Jewish students from schools.
Ordinance 203/1940	requires all Jewish assets to be registered.
Ordinance 93/1941	decides how Jewish properties are to be distributed.
Ordinance 198/1941, The Jewish Code (270 articles, longer than the constitution itself)	announces a Jew is anyone with at least three Jewish grandparents. confiscates Jewish property. forces Jews to wear the yellow Star, sewn onto the left side of outer garments. authorizes government to expel Jews and resettle them.

Ordinance 153/1941 makes Jews subject
to forced labor.

Constitutional Law 68 gives
sanction
to the Slovak Republic
to expel
or deport
its Jews.

Discovering

We traipse up and down streets
looking for the places you lived.
Reading the code of signs,
an arched door,
a passageway between two houses.
We peer out the backdoor of a bakery.
Here you lived above the courtyard,
goats tethered outside.

The stately house where you were born
with my grandfather's initials engraved
in the yellow mortar.
Now some kind of business,
the word *bizuteria* in red under the windows.
You tell me about the old broom business in the basement.
Your father lost the house during the depression.
(Later my uncle said
my grandfather lost it playing cards)

Mr. Kolbar takes a picture of us.
The building overshadows
our three small figures.

What does this mean for you?
Flooding you with images
that burrow inside.

We pose, your arm around me
in front of the boarded-up *Heder*
where you learned the Hebrew alphabet.
I look towards the camera
but you look beyond

The River

My father can smell the river.
We cross streets,
walk under bridges,
pass a yard cluttered with car remains,
make our way through fields of overgrown grass.

Finally we are here.
The River Sekčov is now small and dirty.
The marks on the shoreline
show its erosion over time.
Not like the mighty flow of water
where my father first learned to swim
and a boy was sucked down by the undertow.

We sit on the banks.
His usual reticence loosened
and he spins story after story.
Running through fields,
chasing mice,
playing with friends.
No mention of graffiti on shop windows
   Jews are bloodsuckers
signs on the playgrounds
   Jews not admitted.

His family lost their house.
Moved beside the army barracks,
a half-a-hour walk then
to the synagogue on *Shabbas*.
I imagine him skipping along that wide boulevard
and everywhere the hatred growing.

I take photos of him
staring meditatively
under the willow tree,
his shadow reaching the bushes behind.

The Trains

The Jewish Office sets up
refugee camps,
collects clothes and supplies,
petitions the President.
He will not stop the transports.

Gisi Fleichmann, Rabbi Frieder and five others
organize the illegal Working Group.
Anything to stop the trainloads.
Which German will bend?
Forty thousand American dollars change hands.
The wheels stop.

Hiding

a parish priest in a village
hides a family in a rectory

    when the soldiers come
    they have slipped away

leaving behind the small houses
slowly ascending the steep cliff side

    they find a cave
    a farmer brings them milk and bread

in the town below
trains are departing again

The Importance of Knowing

I kept waiting
for the story behind the story.

Your sister deported,
you and your brother fled to Hungary
to live with families
with new names and papers.
Your oldest brother braving the underground
to make his way to Palestine,
your parents taken.
Those grinding wheels leaving you
an orphan.

My mind fills in the scenes.
What else is there to know?

Resting Ground

I've always liked cemeteries
quiet, gray and white stones
history-embedded inscriptions
contemplative willow trees

months later
mourners come
to unveil the tombstone
place pebbles carefully on the grave

you want to talk to her
or feel close to him

I don't have a cemetery to visit

Unveiling

On Sunday morning,
my father and I come to the synagogue again.
The iron gate leading into the courtyard
is padlocked now.

We stare into the synagogue grounds.
In a house above us
I see a curtain fluttering.
A window shuts.

My father speaks quietly.
He tells me
the town's Jews
were rounded up here
in the courtyard.

I imagine him pinned against
the exterior wall of the synagogue
between his brother and sister,
staring at the Hlinka Guard
surrounding them.

But was he already in Hungary
disguised as a happy-go-lucky kid
playing ball in the schoolyard?

"I could tell you many stories," he says.
He doesn't.

Haviva Reik

How did you feel, Haviva,
when they dropped you from the plane?
You released your parachute
and began that dark descent.
Did you feel chilled by fear? Thrilled by danger?
Did you enjoy those few minutes floating,
that sensation of freedom,
the air cold against your skin?

When you landed on the airfield,
the ground unfamiliar with rock and bush,
did the resistance fighters
run to greet you?
Were they surprised
when they saw the generous curves
of your body, your brown hair
plastered against your head?

Back in your native Slovakia now,
you organized a huge kitchen,
ladling out soup to thousands of desperate Jews.
You helped children escape to Hungary, rescued jettisoned pilots.
When the Germans invaded, the Jewish partisans retreated,
built a camp in the mountains.
As you stood watch, shivering in the unyielding darkness
did you feel forsaken by the stars?

They captured you.

And in the hush of the Kremnica forest,
the sun not yet bathing the trees in light,
among those silent sentinels,
the Germans shot you.

Aunt Marta

You were sixteen, oldest of five
you had no idea where
they were taking you

I know you liked to sew

the housekeeper of your school
hid photos of your class
in the schoolhouse walls

amid the rows of children
I see you
black and white, tiny

(Ap)peal

> "In deporting the Jews, we have simply acted
> in accordance with the command of God,
> Slovak get rid of your enemy."
> – Josef Tiso, President of Slovakia, 1942

Did the church bells ring
when Tiso shook Hitler's hand?
When the government passed the Jewish Code
did you cover your hair with a babushka,
walk quickly to the cathedral at the centre of the town,
give praise as you passed the crucifix,
savour the host in your mouth?

Were you comforted by the benediction
as the Nazis invaded the synagogue?
They wrenched the pulpit from its foundation,
while Jews hid in their cellars,
children clutching their mother's hands,
men pulling their beards.

When they rounded up Jews in the courtyard,
did you watch from your window?
When the first of those fifty-seven transports left
metal doors rattling in the wind,
did you wonder where they were going?
Did you believe the lies?

When all the Jews were gone
deported, fled underground,
or fighting from the Tatras overlooking the town,
did the church bells sound a rejoicing peal?
Did they sound melodic,
the trembling of a deeply buried conscience?

What did you do with their menorahs,
their Passover plates stolen from the synagogues,
their clothes, their shoes,
their jewels, their violins?
Did you send them to Prague
for Hitler's museum?

Why weren't there more
like Gejza Fritz or Ján Balko?
Jozef Sivák who protected Jewish teachers,
or Ján Spišiak who saved Jews
from his post in Budapest?

Why a pogrom after the war?
Why leave us out of your tourist books?
Why a statute of Tiso in the Bratislava square?
Why stare at me?
Why?

Departure

Skimming like a fly on
a deep pool of water
I realize the open curtain
reveals only darkness.

Epilogue – Reunion of Jews from Prešov

We will stand in the courtyard.
We will surround that marble memorial.
Elderly men and women will strike
matches against a barbed wire wreath, light six candles.

The Rabbi will recite the Mourner's Kaddish.
The crowd will chime in
amen, amen
amid the clicking of camera shutters.

We will fill the synagogue.
Priests wearing black will sit on a pew.
White candles will form shadows
on the freshly painted walls.

As Mr. Landa blows the Shofar,
the hall will buzz with excited voices.
The story will be told over and over
in Slovak, Hebrew, Yiddish and English.

We will sing
Yiddish and Hebrew melodies.
They will resonate against the walls,
music absent here for fifty years.

Our voices will rise
up towards the dome ceiling
and fill that dark lonely emptiness.

II

Turning the Corner at Dusk

Birth, December 1960

The tree branches heavy with snow
sound and colour muted
as the earth turned inward
replenishing its wisdom

Some fifteen years earlier
the earth helplessly watched
villages of people thrown alive into ditches
screams of open mouths suffocated

The charred ashes, a cloak on the earth's surface
have intermingled now with the soil
and my parents travelled the ocean
to build lives far from that world

I came tumbling out of that inner universe
my tiny lungs taking in the first gulp of air
the nurse presented me to my mother
"It's a girl!"

I looked satisfied (my mother now reminisces)
untroubled by my journey
through moist enveloping walls
out into the florescent delivery room

My big sister slept fitfully near my father
whom they sent home from the hospital
My mother held me, full of new life
her body still frozen

and I brought the wisdom
of the earth's sedimentary layers
rock-old intuition in my soul
kindness to protect its hibernating animals

I carried too the Jewish sorrow of the age
How could I escape it?
I, the next generation
knew you could die under the bright winter sun

but as I cuddled in my mother's arms
nourishing snow began to fall
flakes whirling and twirling
with the ecstasy of a *hora* dance.

Snapshot

Two girls holding hands
on a balcony or an upstairs deck.
My sister, more serious,
looks intently at the camera,
her stance confident,
arms firm by her side.

I stand slightly behind her.
I look dopey,
my mind somewhere else,
like I'm happy to hold her hand
and take things as they come.

We're both in dresses with short sleeves,
two bows at her waist, one at my neck.
Uneven bangs frame our faces.
My sister's leotards loose and baggy around her ankles,
my legs bare above socks.

The sadness I feel now.
And I wonder when things changed,
or was the black and white camera too primitive
to catch the hidden rays?

Henriette

Black and white photo of three sisters,
you, the youngest, stand out in beauty
long eyelashes framing big, unsure eyes.

Those eyes must have been scared-wide
when your mother – my grandmother –
dropped you off at that Munich orphanage
retrieved you, then left you again.
That rejection always
a red-hot hurt compressing your heart.

Those long six years when in night's closeness
you were moved from one French Jewish
children's refuge to another.
No wonder you always jumped at ambulance sirens,
looked behind in fear.
I never knew where those sounds took you,
far from our treed street where children
skipped rope on front driveways.

No warm caring until Madame and Monsieur Mar,
encouraged at Sunday services,
welcomed you onto their farm
in a valley near Montélimar.
Guided by their Protestant faith,
they named you Henriette,
and when the Nazis came searching,
they kept you safe within old stone walls.

That farm lived for me
in the white nougat
Madame Mar sent us.
Every year, it arrived in a brown paper package
taped up carefully by old skilled fingers.
We ripped it open impatiently
and plunged into that gooey sweetness.

Memory, 1972

In the Zellers store on Princess Street,
I discover the rack of name stickers.
Spin it around and around
until a neon flash of happy-go-luckiness
stops before me.
Psychedelic purple, florescent orange,
"Vote Jackie," "Far-Out Jackie" and "I dig Jackie"
they call.
This celebration of my "Jackiness," a surprise
among the other more popular names: Debbie, Susan and Kathy.

My sister watches as I finger the package
she, a weighted-down "Irene"
named after our grandmother, taken by the Nazis.

Just one more shopping outing,
my mother, sister and I sit at the snack counter.
Mummy buys me a chocolate milkshake,
nods to her waistline,
and orders a piece of coconut cream pie.

When we get into our navy-blue Ford,
my sister presents me with the stickers, "Surprise!"
The two of them beam with that knowing pleasure
of a gift well-chosen,
and my cup runneth over
like in the old psalm they read
over the school broadcast system.

Not long after, my grandfather dies
and a haze settles over our house.
My mother sits on our porch
and stares out into the distance.
And I walk once more
in that shadowed valley.

Therapy

You ask me
what I am feeling today.
Without thinking, I answer
"Despair."
You blink.

Somewhere though, I remember
two little girls crouched
on a bed against the wall.
Moonlight filtering through blue seersucker curtains,
the cat hidden under the bed, ears flattened.
Suddenly a crash, glass splintering, furious shouts.

"Is there anything else there?"
Your calm voice brings me back.
My hands grip the sides of the chair.
It's so hot in this room.

Slipping in deeper
at the back of my head
flies, stench,
skulls with gold fillings extracted.

Turning the Corner at Dusk

I didn't know that was you –
this long grey week,
sinking me deeper and deeper into a green rotting swamp.

So hidden,
you, that despairing child
pushed away, ignored.

But tonight, I can see you
between the darkness and the light
under an old-fashioned street lamp.

A small child
face stained with tears,
a flood that won't stop.

You don't know
that this moment will pass
because all you see ahead
are the closed backs of children
and all you hear
are the hard, angry shouts of three-in-the-morning words
and the smattering of dishes against linoleum floor.
And that loss makes you
cry that much harder.

There is no one to tell you
a garden of flowers and trees waits for you.
Two children giggling,
swaying back and forth on a double wooden swing.

They're holding a place for you
and they will accept you
with your hand-me-down clothes, accented immigrant parents,
your Slavic, Semitic looks –
they will accept you.

I'll take your hand
and I'll lead you out.

Herbie

One camping summer
I decided to call everything "Fred."
The tent was Fred.
My mother was Fred.
Fred was tacked on to every word:
a sandwich-fred, a towel-fred.

My mother laughed
and even my father who spoke slowly with scientific precision,
smiled at his new name.
And I soaked in that playfulness,
giddy with the lightness I had created.

Next summer,
everyone became Harry and then Charlie
and soon it was Herbie,
and so I broke out and stretched our reality
like a clown's wide, red smile.

Today, on the phone
my mother calls me "Herbie"
and ever so briefly, we recall
those moments when we ventured
and names became joy.

Nuclear Family Panic

In those moments
when panic
takes me back   there

        my socked feet slipping on shiny pine stairs
        that angry wave on my heels
        flinging myself on the bed,
        I dialled my best friend's number
        tears salting the heavy, black receiver

In those moments
I have to talk to you

I rush down the street
looking for a phone
breath rabbit-fast
thoughts racing

In those moments
I lose   my confident footing
I forget
the array of city lights from the plane window
I forget
how you pull me close
and look intently in my eyes

I have to talk to you

Your calm
the scent of freshly mown grass
your assurance
the everydayness of drinking
cranberry juice, sitting at our table

and my breathing slows
and I settle back into myself.

Children of Holocaust Survivors

We gather together
pass around the *Yartzeit* candle,
stare into the flame,
call up faces from black and white photographs.
The wind presses against the window behind us.
The fire in the stone fireplace now jewelled embers.

Even in our names
we become the lost.
In each other's stories, we glimpse familiar fragments,
recognize the intensity in our gaze.

We carry the sorrow of our parents,
their strength is passed to us.
We are their resistance.
In our art, we draw
yellow paths beckoning us forward
but the red burning trees
pull us back.

I carry those stories with me.
At the Seder table,
friends and family praise the Warsaw martyrs.
These fighters are our grandparents.
Their souls are with us,
hovering around the light of the Passover candles.
We don't need to open the door
and pray for them to enter.
They are with us.
They are in our boisterous chorus
as we sing the *Chad Gad Ya*.
They are in the sweetness
of the children's off-key song,

in the sadness in eyes,
in my father's silence.

They rejoice
as we rise to sing their anthem
with all our rallied strength.
Hirsh Glick's voice is ours as we sing his marching words.
We are hiding in the woods with him.
We are here! Mir zaynen do!
We are blowing up Nazi trains, fighting with stolen guns.
Mir zaynen do!
We are holding on.

Memorial, Paris

In the Jewish quarter of *le Marais*
a small inconspicuous building.
I ring the bell and I'm frisked in the lobby.
I pay my francs to the woman at the desk.

Through glass doors, I see
a monument in a small courtyard.
Round like a cauldron,
names etched in a never-ending circle,
Auschwitz, Dachau, Treblinka.
The sculpture shines the blue-black of bruises
against the Paris sky.

The doors to the courtyard are locked.
I sit on a hard chair and stare through the windows.
On a bulletin board, newspaper clippings
about a survivor searching for her family,
a drawing of Rachel crying for her children.

Trees shelter the small yard.
Beside black wrought iron benches hangs
a mural of Jews praying and dancing.
Beyond the wooden fence, the bustle of streets,
here only stillness.

Returning to the desk,
I tell the woman,
C'est beau.
She surveys my windbreaker, my running shoes.
Beau? Pas tellement.
She pats her hair, straightens her glasses.
C'est bon, les Jeunes viennent au memorial.
Ils se souviennent.

I want to tell her
I live with the Holocaust every day.
Loss, an iron bolt, weighs down my shoulders,
constricts my neck.

I want to tell her
I remember when
I look at my father
and I see a boy
sitting on a bench alone.

I remember when
people talk excitedly
about the fun of genealogy
and I only see Nazi records of names and numbers.

Oui, c'est beau
I tell her
and I reach for the door.

Amsterdam Jewish Museum

Directions in the guidebook and from the tram-driver
and two trams later,
I'm at Jonas Daniel Meijerplein square.
No Stars of David, no stained glass windows,
at the outdoor clothes market,
no one knows where the museum is.

Where are the pushcarts, the stalls,
the women shopping before *Shabbas*
haggling for the best price
for this apron, that flowered blouse,
the bicycles waiting to deliver home
bags of freshly plucked chicken,
vegetables, pickles and chocolates?

Where are the families crossing the square
on their way to synagogue for evening prayers,
men carrying their *tallit* in velvet embroidered bags,
women with their bright-coloured hats?

Finally a small cobblestone alley,
brown stately buildings, door flanked by white pillars.
A guide explains:
follow the arrows through four synagogues
joined with glass passageways.

People walk through the large rooms, file by
silver cups, torah crowns, menorahs, illuminated prayer books.
Tapestries paired with photos of costumed children for *Purim*,
like the pictures of my cousin's children
hanging in their bedrooms.

Visitors slow.
The war exhibit.
An identity card stamped with a J,
letters from embassies denying papers,
the Hollandse Schouwburg theatre
and the Westerbork prison camp.
One hundred thousand Dutch Jews.

Families carrying suitcases they'll soon have to give away.
A mother holds her daughter's hand.
How long will she feel the child's skin?
She vows to keep the child with her no matter what.

I want those Jews back.
I want that child to spin the *driedl*
chortle with glee as she takes the nuts she has won.
I want the old men to light the menorah,
remember that battle
as they stare into the candle flames.
I want that family to breathe the scent of the *etrog*,
the lemon-like fruit of *Succot*
through the boughed roof of the *Succah*,
stars blessing them.

Up narrow steps to the gallery
where women used to pray,
an exhibit of Dutch Jewish artists.
Portraits of community leaders and rabbis,
paintings of weddings, landscapes.
From a woman's self-portrait,
eyes stare at me.

I want those painters back,
mixing colours on their easels,
painting posters for their unions.
Nodding with satisfaction as they get the exact colour,
the exact caption they want.

Through a passageway, up more stairs,
more photos.
Diamond workers cutting tiny stones,
a father and son standing beside their clothing factory
seized during the war.

I want to pass out leaflets
with sisters and brothers,
sit on hard wooden floors, swept into other worlds
by Yiddish poets.
I want to hear the fiddling of an old Klezmer tune,
stamp my foot, circle round and round.
I want to hear their breath
beside me now.

My tour ends in the cafeteria,
a tea and some gefilte fish.
An elderly man and woman speak in Hebrew.
I buy postcards in the gift shop.
I'll take the tram
to the hotel, pack my bag
for tomorrow's flight.

Now I take
one last look in the sanctuary
the big arched windows
high blue ceiling.

Autumn Reflection

Blue-grey rings under my eyes
greet me in the mirror.
All that beckons ahead
are grey filing cabinets
and the muted computer screen.

I am weighed down with
the loneliness of seasons changing
and the end of sky-blue summer companionship.
The sadness of overcast clouds
and I project my awareness out
overwhelmed by despair.

Remembering arriving home
to silence in empty apartments.
Before, lonely walks in deserted parks,
dressed in the bleakness of a birthday forgotten.
Earlier still,
shut out from playground games,
the scolding at my scream when
the lash of a skipping rope burned my eye.
The hard brick against my forehead when
I ran into the schoolyard wall
and the surprising caring after.

A wind whips up around me,
scatters leaves, burying fall's glory
on the grey pavement.

Yom Kippur in Kensington Market

We rent the community centre on Cecil Street
for High Holiday services.
Once a synagogue of Polish Jews
the Ostrovtzer shul.
Down the street, the Jewish Old Folks Home,
and on Spadina, the storefront union offices,
Hyman's Book and Art Shop, United Bakers,
and Walerstein's Ice Cream Parlour.
The *schmatah* business in one run-down building after another,
basements and lofts where Jews sweated
over sewing machines and press irons.

Now, brick houses painted red
cohabit with Chinese restaurants
where we dine on hot and sour soup and Shanghai noodles.

In the community centre, the *Aron Hakodesh* holds the Torah.
Silk screen prints hang from the balcony
where women and children used to sit.

We can't let these holy days go by
without doing something.
We come looking.
Thumping our chests, we confess
Ashamnu, bagadnu, gazalnu, dibarnu dofi,
he-evinu, v'hirshanu, zadnu
We continue, "We have been negligent; we have betrayed;
we have robbed; we have slandered;
we have been perverse; we have been wicked."

Struggling with the idea of the Judging King,
I look up to the towering chandelier,
gold Stars of David engraved in its base.
My spirit shoots up between the stars,
hovers above the congregation below.

As the solemn notes of the *Avinu Malkeynu*
rise from the yearning people below,
I hear the whispers of the old community prayers,
the cantor's passionate *Kol Nidre* plea
people would come from miles to hear.

I hear the rise of two women's voices
as they recount Emma Goldman's speech
at the Labour Lyceum last week.
There's the rustle of *Der Kampf*
as a man reads it between the pages of his prayer book.
A woman in a green dress with a starched white collar
whispers to the woman beside her
about the last meeting of the Workmen's Circle.

Outside there's the musty smell of dry autumn leaves.
A man in a black overcoat passes handbills around
to see the play, *Eight Men Speak*.
He cries, "only the Progressive Arts Club
would dare to take on this subject
– arrested for being a communist, here in Canada!
Come to the Standard Theatre, next Sunday."
On the steps, men and women complain about Superior Cloak
and there's the stir of people
talking union.

My spirit hovers above all of this
momentarily, then I'm back in my body.
The rainbow *Kippah* has fallen off the man's head in front of me,
I hand it to him
as the Rabbi tells us to rise for the *Amidah* prayer.

Journey to the Funeral of Lois Heitner (1957–1993)

From the train window
I see a calf in a field nearby.
A mother cow nuzzles her young.
Your new baby,
no longer soothed by your sonorous voice.

You will not take him to school,
declaring you were his mother too.
You would have revelled in
challenging the principals, teachers
like you challenged us all.
Your last living gesture,
shielding your baby with your body
as the car rolled upside down
and the mass of steel threatened to crush both of you.

>   train whistles
>   landscape sails by
>   wheels rolling, rolling

Fifty years ago,
our ancestors on a train.
Life enmeshed with death.
We talked about our history.
How my burden was heavier
but you too carried the pain.

You had the look so right.
One dangling earring, the clip in your ear
purple clothes, large silver rings.
How many other women came out
because you made it look so good?

      the train whistles
      landscape sails by
      wheels rolling, rolling

Now we approach
the city of your death, my hometown.
Three days in that barren hospital room,
your lover down the hall,
the wakeful women surrounding you like flowers.

      the train whistles
      the landscape sails by
      wheels rolling, rolling

We stop in Cornwall.
A woman and a man
pace up and down the train.
When they find their son,
they flash a sign, mouth words through the glass.
Your family stretched beyond this landscape.
The children all around you
mourned your loss.

Soon we will chant prayers over you,
the last time I will *daven* with you
in a ceremony you would not have liked,
we women forced into do-nothing roles.
We will place you in the earth
to return.

Epiphany by Chikanishing Creek

I wait for you by the car.
The huge rocks gleaming pink,
hugging the creek below.

In my rainbow tank top, my baseball hat on backwards,
I start bopping to that song,
I have annoyed you with the whole canoe trip.

You come back
and smile at me swaying,
the Jack Pines towering behind.

In that moment,
My value flashes before me and
I wonder if I can hold on to that sense

of me
swinging my hips in the warm sun,
surrounded by the pink Canadian Shield.

Seesaw

at one end   of the seesaw
a child grips   the side of the board
her mother reads   on the park bench
the child cries   the mother watches
an older child   high on the swings.

at the other end   a woman sits
she holds the hand   of a blond-haired woman
encircling them,   a group of men and women
eat cake,   do the chicken dance
Hava Nagilah   they shout.

in the middle, I crouch
the weight comes down.

I slide to the girl   her sadness engulfs me
I wave at the mother   she smiles at the older child

the weight shifts

I slide towards the woman   I watch the group dancing
a big toothy smile   flashes across my face.

the weight comes down

at the fulcrum
desperately
I try to stay centred

using my elbows, my arms
I hoist myself to my knees
I pull my weight up

                    for a second
                    I'm standing
                    arms in the air

the end comes down   I start to slide again

            I know now it's possible
                    to stand.

In the Closet with My Relatives on the French Riviera

There are no mirrors
in this small retirement town.
Only he and she in matching T-shirts
pushing baby strollers along the boardwalk.
No women buzzed by the local barber in jeans and leather jackets,
trying to catch my eye.
No men walking two by two, rolling their hips from side to side.

On the beach, the rock barrier juts out into the sea.
I listen to the waves, receding
one stone at a time, milky lather rushing over the pebbles,
the water opaque,
blue and green expanse surrounds me, fills me.

I escape my aunt and uncle's small apartment
walk under the narrow stone overpass,
skirting the dog droppings,
houses enclosed by neatly trimmed bushes, pungent with growth.
Crossing the main road, I join the couples
promenading on the boardwalk,
men and women, arm in arm, talking quickly.
I walk past them.
My stride protests that femininity.
My nylon windbreaker challenges their fashionable wool jackets.

I climb down the cement stairs,
leaving the paved walkway behind, scramble on giant boulders.
My running shoes find their footing.
The moon almost full reflects in the still water.
The sea separates me from home
where I walk openly with my pink triangles, my rainbow
tra-la-la necklace, home, where I do not have to hide.

My uncle drives me to the train station for my outing in Nice,
telling me not to get my haircut there,
saying I should go to my aunt's hairdresser.
I want to know, but don't dare ask,
"Does she know how to give a good dyke cut?"
I laugh uncomfortably
when he teases me about hugging a boyfriend
instead of my cat.

My grandmother asks if there are places in Toronto
to meet single men.
At the synagogue for Yom Kippur
my grandmother asks the rabbi's wife
to help her find me a husband.
"Husbands for all Israel's daughters"
they croon together joyously.
They pray for the new year
"Peace for all the children of Israel."

On the beach, I vow to the moon:
I want to be as insistent as the waves pounding,
erode old hatreds through persistent relentless force.

I want to hold a giant mirror to the world.
See a man and woman smile at two men in a tonguing kiss
see two women with short hair
push a two-year-old in a stroller
as an elderly woman coos over the child.

And there I am
dancing on a boulder
hair shaved close to my head
a labrys swinging merrily from my ear.

III

The Oceans Part and Out You Come

Wishing for a Child

I wish on the Pacific Ocean,
the foamy trail receding behind the ferry.
I wish on the tide pools
full of tiny crabs, shells and seaweed,
perfect for children to splash in.

I wish.
I squeeze my hands,
close my eyes tight.
I wish on the wag
of the golden retriever's tail.

I wish on the duck's bum
stuck up as it dives for food.
I wish on the V-formation
of the Canada geese.

I wish on my dream to ride a horse
although I'm afraid of heights.
I wish on my parents' determination
to wallpaper the kitchen, raise children
with little to draw on but scars.

I wish on my body's strength
to overcome its aches and fears,
grow a new life
and push that life out.

Surely all this is more powerful
than a twinkling little star.

Aviva

I

They start Wednesday.
Sometime in the night
like menstrual cramps deep in my vulva
my body beginning
its ancient rhythmical journey.

By Thursday morning,
I am on the phone,
massaging and kneading my groin.
"No, not close together
Yes, I'll call you."

At six o'clock
half an hour before the swimming pool closes,
I grab a cab.
"Is it a boy or a girl?" he asks
and like everyone else, gives his prediction.

Other swimmers pass me, as I back crawl down my lane,
the contractions invisible,
this internal beauty only known to me.
When the lifeguard blows the whistle,
I pull my swollen body up the steps.

Walking in the warm twilight,
Gerrard Street, busy with people and the whirl of streetcars.
At the park, girls in red and white uniforms chase a soccer ball.
Parents cheer them from folding chairs on the grass
and the buses wait to bring them all home.

II

I will teach you
how to listen for the robin's evening song.
I will teach you to observe the quiet sparrows
sunbathing in the pavement dust.
I will show you how to approach cats,
slowly with your hand outstretched,
never come up quickly and surprise a dog.
How to greet the man in the store
who doesn't understand English,
and how to talk to the woman at the party
who sits on the couch by herself.

I will teach you what I know

and I will tell you over and over again
how you came to me.

III

After the pressure comes release
the hypnotist told us.
My partner's fingers gouge
my foot, distracting me
until the mucous plug blazes out in a red streak
and lies like a grey worm on the bed.

All night the hypnotist's tape
plays over and over again.
We doze between the contractions,
sharp pain pulls me out of the trance.
"Don't leave me"
I tell her.

The midwife shows me how to breathe.
"Hoo, hoo"
I chant like a sick owl
all the way to the hospital
in the grey early morning rush hour.
"Take Shuter Street," I tell her
"I have to push."
She watches me through the rear-view mirror.
"Don't!" she says.
And more chanting
propels me forward

until I am squatting on
the delivery table,
a weightlifter poised to pick up the bar
leg strength concentrated.
Pushing down with all my might
deep belly grunts, groans
pushing past those violating fingers
from many years ago.
I am Amazon, I am Artemis,
I am Joan of Arc.

And the crown of your head
sears my perineum
and everything stretches and tears
like continents shifting and coming together again
and the oceans part and out you come
all arms and legs
and I feel your warm slippery body
against my belly.

My Body Has Turned Utilitarian

Breasts, no longer erogenous landscape
for nibbling, caressing, sucking hard.
Nor to jiggle on the Riviera's pebbly beaches
or to bounce freely at women's music festivals.

My breasts are now
the source of life, no less.
Their nourishment has created cells
of brown soft hair, muscle chunks and baby fat.
They are a sleep potion, a soother, even a laxative
and yes, I'll bare them
in the shopping mall, in the restaurant
wherever and whenever
fussing, fidgeting and that small voice whine
signal hunger.

Warrior marks decorate my stomach.
The tree of life
spreading upward and outward across my shrunken belly.
Fingers are for massaging sore gums,
rubbing cream into baby leg and bum crevices.
Palms comfort a tired cheek,
provide a passage through which
the land of sleep can safely be entered.
Hands wring out cotton diapers,
and wash her face with petite yellow and blue face cloths.

Shoulders provide resistance
to push out a burp,
a solid rest for a small head to peer over.
Arms and legs carry sixteen pounds of baby weight.
Hair is for little hands to pull and explore.
I shake it and squeals of laughter spill everywhere.

Vanity is gone, grooming minimal,
and yet the mirror shows
my contented face
and her happy-go-lucky, two-teeth smile.

Attachment

It's sensing when you're crying from one floor away,
knowing you need to nurse
when I'm in the next building
and I can barely sit in my class,
wondering how fast I can get to you.

It's the milky scent of my grey nightgown,
the snugness of socks slid over hands
because you just won't keep them under the blankets.
It's the reach of your arms for me,
your trill when I hold you upside down,
your squeal when I tickle your neck.
It's the way you fall asleep, stretched out on my lap
on that brown couch in the waiting room.
Wherever we are, you know you're home.

It's your satisfied smile
when I have understood your hungry cues.
When we lie at night, side by side,
your breathing slows to mine
and we drift together into dreams
like two ducks riding a wave crest.
You inch towards me in sleep,
and I wake to feel your body pressed up against mine.

It asks of me,
no, it demands of me
to be resourceful, patient, creative,
to entertain you with silly songs,
to be your own private cheerleader.
To hold on to my rope end,
and you'll decide
whether the tension is taut
or slack.

Diaper Rash

On the day before our anniversary, we argue
about how to treat diaper rash.
You, the anti-pharmaceutical, herbs and homeopathic advocate,
want to continue with the cream of beeswax,
sweet almond oil and comfrey.
I say it is time to see
what the allopathic world can offer.

When our plans for a weekend getaway dissolve
in teething, colds and a raw, red bottom,
I know motherhood has really set in.

Six years of working things out and the occasional
put-up-the-dukes, hands-waving-in-the-air argument, pay off.
You agree to a visit to the hospital doctor,
and by five o'clock the next day we have the prescription.
(Four days later, the pimply smarting redness still persists)

We head out for a romantic dinner on Church Street.
A female impersonator cries at the next table,
while the bartender, father-proud, flashes photos
and tells us about one of his customers
asking him to donate sperm.

Our baby tastes the crisp white of the napkin,
crackles the paper tablecloth under her fingers.
I glow with the Australian Chardonnay,
this chance to fill my constantly empty, still-feeding-two body.
Your pleasure in my indulgence gives me
that tucked-in-at-night feeling.

And in the frost edged windows, I can see the reflection
of that evening, six years ago,
when you announced your feelings, over wine,
cold feet in our boots in the Tree House,
where now men drink creamy lattes in the Church Street Starbucks.

No roses to carefully place in a vase, no climax of hot panting sex.
Instead, you massage the golf-ball size knot in my neck.
Later when I nurse the baby to sleep,
I hear two rhythms of breath beside me,
and snuggling down in the depths of our king-size bed
I know everything is just right.

Bath Time

You gently massage the shampoo
of coconut oil, fennel and chamomile,
into our daughter's hair
and begin the never-ending task of combing out
those split-ended tangles.
Knots from too much time in winter hats
pressed against the navy-blue nylon stroller.

In your careful strokes
I see generations of women
lovingly brushing their children's hair.
Mother's knowledge passed on
through that invisible lifeline.

"This is impossible"
you grumble under your breath.
"We should get her hair cut"
you threaten,
something we are both reluctant to do.

She happily dunks her red and yellow plastic boat
and pours water on her legs.
The green frog with white spots and the orange starfish
merrily float at the other end of the tub.
Mama rubber duck and four baby ducks
bob above the still-lingering suds of lavender bubble bath.
"Guck, Guck," she says
identifying this favourite bird.

"There," you say triumphantly.
Her brown hair, now waves
of soft wet curls.
Our little Rapunzel
ready for bed.

Mapping

When your labour started,
I became your body's cartographer
to guide us through the passages, hills and coves
of that journey from night to dawn and dawn once more
and finally the afternoon sun.

I didn't know
I could map your body.
Abuse etched in its memory.

I told the midwife
your fear of tightness around your neck
and to stay away from your belly button,
as she pressed her Doppler on that taut globe,
listening to that strong heartbeat.

When your wish for a tranquil home birth
transformed into a
"Get me to the hospital, quick,"
I cheered you on
as the car moved through the sleek, humid streets.

To the doula, I said
to keep you watered,
thirsty for too long
in your childhood desert-house
where a father and a mother never spoke
and the silences exploded.
He broke your mother's back,
the police came and left,
and always you crept to your bed
along that long brown hallway,
terrified of what awaited you.

In the hospital room,
we rested on blankets on that hard floor,
and when morning sun
brought its hope into that orange room
but still no baby, I consoled you.

You carefully pulled your tired and heavy body
on to the stretcher and
I held your hand.
When the doctor placed the oxygen mask
over your face,
I guided your breath
to keep away that terror of suffocating,
as you relaxed your feet, then legs,
then arms, then hands.

Your mountains and gullies,
ancient underground streams,
knowledge you can't tap.

When finally the doctor
pulled her out of your belly
and you strained to see her,
asking, scared, if she was all right,
and that being of light and strength
let out a loud shrieking cry,
I neatly folded my map.

Maya

Before the rhythms of birth took over
I stood in our backyard
looking out at the hazy summer night.
A presence hovered in the air
like a rose, a fragrance sweetening the night's stillness.
I knew finally the sex of that baby
who had taken over all of your body
until you had no energy left.

After thirty-two hours of wrenching contractions
two epidurals and still no baby,
the doctor finally
pulled that strong, stuck, nine-pound body
out of your belly.

"Look, it's a boy!" he called.
A second of surprise as I digested this news,
then,
"No, she's a girl!"

And as she was washed and weighed,
Little Maya opened her tiny mouth
and let out a wail
so deafening
the doctor told us,
she had the loudest baby cry
she had ever heard.
And joyful and tentatively hopeful all at once,
I waited for my turn
to hold her.

Excavating Again

I couldn't find the right time
to call you,
so I waited until the last possible minute.
You answered the call at your office,
the sound of your professional voice
threatening to shake my resolve.

But with Baby Maya's naming ceremony,
only three days away,
I needed to know.
What could I say about her namesake,
this aunt I had never known?

You were quiet.
What you offered, a few adjectives.
Before I could respond,
I heard you crying enormous sobs,
that old grief engulfing you.

Later you read me a poem you wrote
as you paced between those limestone buildings.

A Tribute to Marta Buncel
by Erwin Buncel

She was lovely in spirit.
Only goodness flowed from her face,
with a trace of a smile Mona-Lisa like,
and gifted she was too,
less than eighteen years old,
and an accomplished seamstress already.
At the *B'nai Akiba* evening gatherings,
she sang and danced joyfully.

In goodness of heart,
she came forth from hiding
when they came to fetch Mother.
Alas, it was in vain
as they took both.

Now little Maya has come to us,
as a gift from God.
She brings to us joy.
May she walk in happiness
in the long years of her life.

Family

Sometimes I crave the freedom
of *la vie sans enfants*.
Coming home at whatever time,
my day to shape as I please.

I miss movies, dances,
meeting a friend for a bite to eat.
No worries about time and
little faces waiting eagerly for bedtime stories.

But today, I am swimming
and I see two small figures
making sandcastles on the beach.
The bigger one looks up and I wave

and she waves back
and that little hand connects me
and I am happy.
And still complaining,
I trade my freedom over and over again
for this.

Whining

In daycare centres around the country,
is it surreptitiously passed from child to child?
One child whispers the secret code to another
and the exact tone is transmitted
from mouth to ear, from mouth to ear.

At home that night,
at the dinner table
the child tries out her newly acquired skill.
"I don't want to eat ___"
Whatever is on her plate.

The mother looks up surprised.
The words she has heard before, but that tone...
The mother's shoulders involuntarily rise
the forehead wrinkles, the arms tighten,
a look of annoyance passes over her face.

And the child realizes
she is on to something
big and powerful.

The Beach at Sandbanks Park

It's taken hours to get here.
No, weeks of planning, shopping, packing.
Loading up the car with sleeping bags,
diapers, dolls, toys, clothes
and bags and more bags of endless stuff.

As we arrive at the beach
one small hand in mine,
sandalled feet trudging through the sand,
plodding up the steep dune
as hot sand catches between our toes.

Put on swim diapers and Winnie the Pooh swimsuits,
rub sunscreen into arms, legs.
Be careful around the eyes.
Zip up yellow and purple life jackets.

Tiny white and grey shells crunch under our feet
as we run to the water's edge.
I lift two excited dolphins over the waves
with a "whee!" and a "jump!"
They happily squeal.
Then with their pail and shovels poised,
they settle in for some serious sand play.

Finally it's my turn.
I run out, the waves splashing against my legs.
The ridges of sand
give way under my feet.
I skip over the shallow waves
and then I'm in waist deep.
I dive into a wave crest
and as the water gushes around
the light moves past me, purple and blue.

All at once, I'm twelve again
waiting for that perfect wave.
I plunge in, the foam engulfs me.
Then I dive in the next wave and the next,
throw myself backward
and my body slaps the water.

Generation to Generation

How will I tell my children about the camps
when pictures of green Martians scare them?
When these truths become part of them,
will they look at their grandfather and grandmother differently?
Will they hide their Jewishness in shadows?
Will they still wear their difference proudly,
a Star of David pendant on a necklace, silver-bright?

Evocation

When that anger wells up inside of me
and my children become just obstacles in my way
and I blame you for something that is really my fault

When you are late getting home
and I keep going to the door, looking out the window
worrying, worrying, horrible images in my mind

When the phone does not work or the toilet is blocked
and I move into crisis mode, adrenalin flowing
and somehow my life is threatened

When I toss and turn
as arguments play over and over in my mind
and the red numbers of the digital clock keep flashing

I ask "When will this end?"

With all my strength, I call on
the might of Abraham, Isaac and Jacob,
I call on the wisdom of Sarah, Rachel, Rebecca.

I even throw in those other biblical heavy-weights
Miriam, Esther, Naomi and Ruth,
Moses, Mordecai, David and Jonathan.

Come be a barrier
between that damage and my children.
Let them escape my Holocaust past.

Make a dam
to stop that septic tide,
so only clear water passes through.

December Hope

I walk along Carleton Street,
turn into Allen Gardens.
The cityscape glows with window-light.
A crescent moon competes with that brightness
and a string of blue Christmas lights flaps in the wind.

I am escaping pain
pushed down for too long,
until it started erupting hot ash,
molten anger frightening
small crestfallen faces.

Pellets of trauma fall,
hit the paved path around me.
I want to be like the snake
shedding its skin all at once,
but my shifts are subtle, tiny movements.

I walk and I walk
and I imagine
it will heal me,
and at least for now
it does.

Piano Music

This morning, I woke up and heard music,
a sonatina
I used to thump out on the piano.

    Run into the study of my parents' home
    slam the door shut behind me,
    throw open the music book
    and begin to play.

    Play as hard and as loud as I can.
    My rage flowing into
    first trembling, then calmer fingers
    absorbed by the black and white keys.

    Only the rust-coloured blanket
    on my mother's spare bed
    keeps me company.

    Other times
    I snuggle up to her on that couch
    during her afternoon rest,
    both our heads under the blanket,
    my stomach gurgling beside her.

That music comes back today
and I want to search for it and
play it one more time.
I find it in a dusty music book,
a piece by Dussek.
I glance at the framed photos on
the top of my cherry wood piano.
The faces of my children beam.
Their radiance shines over me.

My fingers remember the notes,
the strong forte opening, the quick crescendo.
The chords, less discordant now,
the sweetness of the treble, less painful.

Divining

In the negative spaces
that you can't see or touch
the memories live on.
They reach out from their
subterraneous homes,
the dark recesses of awareness.

    A child stomps her feet.
    "Believe me, believe me"
    she cries.
    She talks of karate hands threatening to box ears,
    and of being car-trapped, surrounded by angry words.
    No loving fingers briskly warmed her frozen toes.
    No one sheltered her from the shadow worms
    that striped her hands in the night
    and the snakes that chased her in dreams.

    And always that well of disappointment
    that got deeper and deeper.

Now your care brings forth
those absences.
You are my divining rod.
My hands hold on to your intuitive knowing
and you lead me, sometimes doubtful
but always hopeful,
to those trapped hidden places.
Together we find water,
and in releasing it,
it flows strong and clean.

Historical Notes

In the 1930s, about 4,000 Jews lived in Prešov, Slovakia, which represented one quarter of the total population. A rich Jewish cultural, social and religious life existed in the town. There were several synagogues and many Jewish associations such as the Girl's Association Deborah, the Prešov Jewish Industrial and Workshop Association and the Neological Cultural Association. Sports activities were organized by the Makabi Physical Training Club. The Jewish Museum Association was very active both in Prešov and beyond the East Slovakia region.

With the start of World War II, the numbers of Jews in Prešov increased at the end of the 1930s as the town became a shelter for persecuted Jews from Germany, Austria, Bohemia, Moravia and Poland. Prešov was the first town in Slovakia where anti-Jewish regulations were imposed such as the compulsory wearing of the yellow ribbon, which was later replaced by the yellow Star of David. Jews were banished from their flats on the main street and Jewish property was confiscated.

The first transportation of young Jewish girls to concentration camps took place on March 25, 1942. About 500 Jews escaped to Hungary and from there, some escaped to Palestine. Jews joined the partisan groups and many of them died in the fighting. More than 6,000 Jews were transported from Prešov and its surrounding area to their death in concentration camps. Only about 800 Jews from Prešov survived the war.

After the war, the remaining Jews struggled to re-establish the community, including helping the survivors of the concentration camps and reviving Jewish religious and social activities. In 1997, the Orthodox synagogue was painted and renovated and Jews from Prešov now living around the world were invited to a reunion. A few hundred people attended this event, filling the synagogue and overflowing into the courtyard. Dezider Landa, a leader of the Jewish community in Prešov, has worked tirelessly to preserve the history of the Prešov Jews.

A more comprehensive and complete explanation can be found in *Stručné Dejiny Prešovských Židov* by Peter Kónya and Dezider Landa, Prešov 1995, 113–120.

Notes on the Poems

"Haviva Reik"

Haviva Reik was a Slovakian Jew whose original name was Marta. She emigrated to Palestine and later enlisted in the Palmach, a Jewish underground military organization. The British Special Operations Executive asked the Palmach for people who knew Central Europe who could parachute into enemy territory and establish contact between the British army and the Jewish Slovakian resistance fighters. Reik volunteered for this task. She took wireless and paratrooper courses. Reik waited in Italy with three other parachutists to be dropped into Slovakia. But the British authorities refused to send a woman behind enemy lines. Reik wouldn't give up her mission and she hitched a ride with an American military transport bound for the Slovakian town of Banaska Bystrica, reaching the site before her male counterparts.

"(Ap)peal"

Josef Tiso was President of Slovakia during the war years.

Jewish Code was a group of anti-Jewish laws modelled after the Nuremberg laws (e.g. denying Jews the right to own property, denying them basic civil rights).

Hitler's museum refers to his orders that the synagogues in Prague be saved to collectively become a museum for an extinct race. Jewish cultural objects seized from the Czech Jewish population were sent there.

Dr. Gejza Fritz was the Minister of Justice in Slovakia and he ensured that the courts were lenient towards Jews.

Dr. Ján Balko was a member of parliament who presented a motion to the President and the government protesting the deportations.

Dr. Jozef Sivák, as the Minister of Education during the war, used his power to warn the Jewish leaders about upcoming deportations and ensured that no letters of protection were revoked from Jewish teachers, thereby protecting Jewish schoolteachers from deportation for as long as possible.

Ján Spišiak was the Slovak ambassador in Budapest who gave Slovakian passports to Slovak Jews who had fled to Hungary without identification and needed to return to Slovakia when Jews in Hungary were no longer safe. He also issued thousands of letters of protection to Slovak Jews.

"Children of Holocaust Survivors"

Hirsh Glick was a resistance fighter and poet who wrote a song called *Zog Nit Keyn Mol* (translated as "Never Say!"). This song became an anthem of the resistance movement.

"Amsterdam Jewish Museum"

Jonas Daniel Meijerplein is the centre of the old Jewish quarter of Amsterdam.

Hollandse Schouwburg theatre was an assembly point in Amsterdam from which Jews were deported.

Westerbork was an internment camp in the east of Holland.

"Yom Kipper in Kensington Market"

Ostrovtzer shul was a vibrant Jewish synagogue for more than three decades from the 1920s to the 1950s in what is now the Cecil Street Community Centre.

Eight Men Speak was a play which defended the eight leaders of the Communist party who were arrested under a section of the criminal code prohibiting advocacy of violent overthrow of the government.

Superior Cloak was a notorious factory which in 1934 moved to Guelph to escape strikers. Strikers followed the factory to Guelph. The strike lasted about 10 weeks and was so successful that the company was forced to return to Toronto.

Glossary of Terms and Phrases

Amidah: a prayer said standing, recited often silently at all three daily prayers.

Aron Hakodesh: ark, cabinet where the Torah is stored during services.

Ashamnu, bagadnu, gazalnu, dibarnu dofi he-evinu, v'hirshanu, zadnu: these words are taken from a prayer for Yom Kippur called "Ashamnu: An Alphabet of Wrongdoing" in which Jews itemize our wrong-doings from the previous year with each sin starting with a different letter of the alphabet.

Avinu Malkeynu: a prayer repeated frequently in the Rosh Hashanah and Yom Kippur services, means, "Our Forgiving Parent, Our Sovereign."

Chad Gad Ya: popular Passover song.

davening: praying, often characterized by swaying.

Der Kampf: "The Struggle," a Yiddish language newspaper that was published by the Labour League, a left-wing Jewish organization.

driedl: spinning top for children for Hanukkah.

etrog: a citrus fruit, part of the Succot celebrations.

Heder: Jewish school for children.

High Holidays: a term used to describe the time period of Rosh Hashanah and Yom Kippur.

Kippah: skullcap.

Kol Nidre: a solemn prayer sung three times at the beginning of Yom Kippur services.

lekech: sweet cake.

Lighting of the Six Candles: a ritual to remember the six million Jews who perished in the Holocaust.

Menorah: candelabra for Hanukkah.

Mir zaynen do: "We are here" in Yiddish.

Mourner's Kaddish: a prayer recited over the passing of loved ones.

Opening the door: a ritual in the Seder when Jews open the door to their house and sing a prayer asking for the prophet Elijah to come inside.

Purim: a holiday where people dress in costumes to celebrate the survival of the Jews from persecution in Persia.

Schmatah business: garment and clothing industry.

Seder: a ceremonial dinner at Passover.

Shabbas (Shabbat): the Jewish Sabbath begins on Friday evening and continues through Saturday until the evening.

Shofar: a ram's horn blown on the High Holidays. Some say the sound symbolizes crying.
Succah: a wooden hut built for Succot. The roof is covered with slats and tree branches so that one can see the night sky shining through.
Succot: a holiday of the harvest, usually in October.
Tallit: prayer shawl.
Torah crowns: decorative silver crowns placed on the scrolls of the Torah.
Yartzeit candle: memorial candle lit annually on the anniversary date of the death of a family member.
Yom Kippur: the Day of Atonement, takes place 10 days after Rosh Hashanah, the Jewish New Year.

Acknowledgements

Some of these poems were previously published in: *CV2*; *Atlantis: A Women's Studies Journal*; *The Amethyst Review*; *Poetica: Reflections on Jewish Thought* and *Kaleidoscope: An International Journal of Poetry*.

Historical information about Jews in Slovakia and specifically Prešov in the Holocaust was gathered from a number of sources. A very helpful reference was, "The Jews of Slovakia: 1939–1945" by Ladislav Lipscher in *The Jews of Czechoslovakia: Historical Studies and Surveys*, volume III, edited by Avigdor Dagan, The Jewish Publication Society of America Philadelphia, Society for the History of Czechoslovak Jews, New York: 1984.

Another helpful source was *Stručné Dejiny Prešovských Židov* by Peter Kónya and Dezider Landa, Prešov: 1995, which documents the history of Jews in Prešov. Information about Haviva Reik was gathered from the Jewish Women's Archive, "Jewish Women and the Feminist Revolution," website, http://jwa.org.

I would like to express my deepest appreciation to Laura Lush for mentoring me with my writing for more than a decade. I am extremely grateful to her for teaching me the finer nuances of the craft of writing, for nurturing my work, sensitively editing these poems and for encouraging me to always go in deeper.

I wish to thank Eric Folsom for his skilled and insightful editing of the manuscript. I greatly appreciate his work in enhancing the beauty of the language and his care and attention to the many details of the writing. Thank you to Noelle Allen and Lindsay Hodder at Wolsak and Wynn for all their support with the process of turning my manuscript into a book. My thanks go to Rachel Rosen for her beautiful design work on the book. Thank you also to Brenda Joy Lem for her creative ideas for the cover design.

I wish to express my gratitude to my parents, Penny and Erwin, for their determination to survive and thrive out of struggle and persecution. I would like to thank my sister, Irene Buncel, for her example of using artistic expression to explore our family stories.

My heartfelt appreciation goes to Sue Guttenstein for encouraging me to pursue my dream and for her caring and steadfast support. I wish to express my thanks to Jen Bayani, Chava Finkler, Ruth Gayle, Ruth Mandel, Lynne Marks, Debra Phelps, Dolores Pitcher, Sarah Pointer, Susan Roller, Sheila Stewart and Greg van Riel for encouraging and supporting me in this project. Aviva Goldberg was my adviser on Jewish rituals, holidays and prayers, and I appreciate her help immensely.

Finally, I cannot express enough appreciation to my partner, Lorraine Gale, for being my writing cheerleader, for always believing in my writing, encouraging me to write and being the first one to hear a new poem with positive and constructive comments. Most of all, I am forever indebted to Lorraine and our two children, Aviva and Maya, for helping me to turn the corner at dusk.

Jacquie Buncel's poetry has been published in journals such as *Fireweed; Atlantis: A Women's Studies Journal; Contemporary Verse Two* and *Poetica: Reflections of Jewish Thought*. Her poetry and short fiction have appeared in a number of anthologies including *Outrage: Dykes and BIs Resist Homophobia* and *Countering the Myths: Lesbians write about the Men in their Lives*. She has an B.A.(Honours) in English Literature from Queen's University and a Masters of Education from the Ontario Institute for Studies in Education of the University of Toronto. She is currently the Executive Director of a non-profit community-based organization that provides social, recreational, and health promotion programs for seniors. She lives in Toronto with her partner and their two children.